Mouse and Me!

3

Student Book

OXFORD
UNIVERSITY PRESS

Written by **Mary Charrington** and **Charlotte Covill**

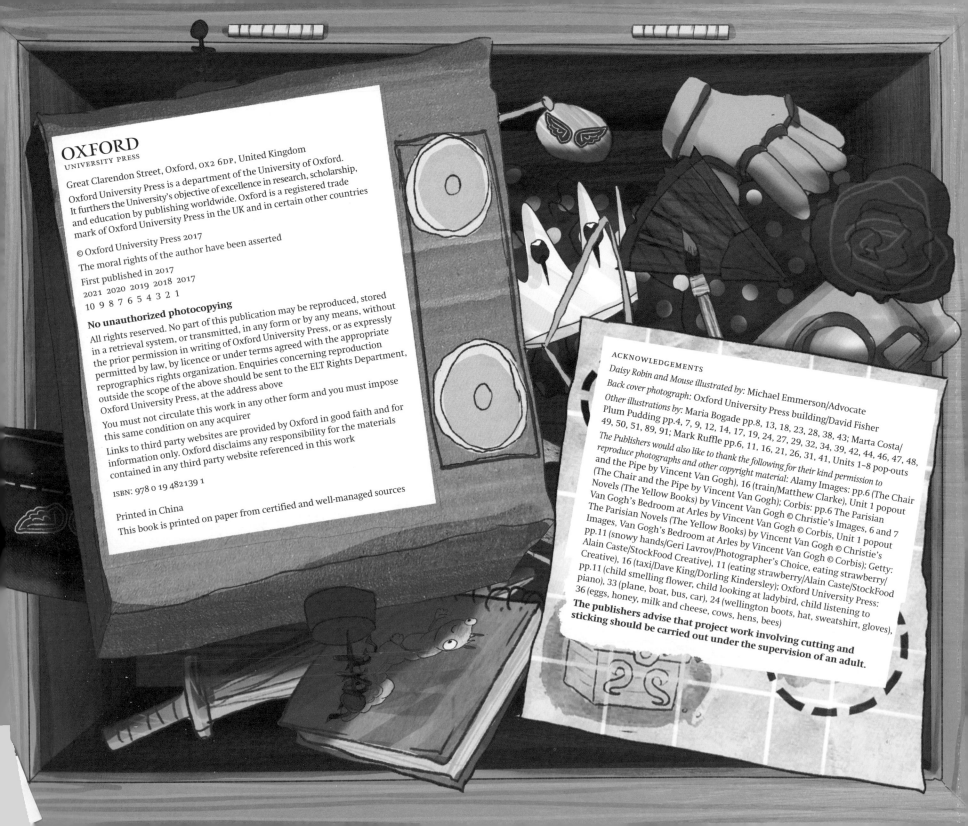

OXFORD
UNIVERSITY PRESS

Great Clarendon Street, Oxford, OX2 6DP, United Kingdom

Oxford University Press is a department of the University of Oxford.
It furthers the University's objective of excellence in research, scholarship,
and education by publishing worldwide. Oxford is a registered trade
mark of Oxford University Press in the UK and in certain other countries

© Oxford University Press 2017

The moral rights of the author have been asserted

First published in 2017

2021 2020 2019 2018 2017
10 9 8 7 6 5 4 3 2 1

ISBN: 978 0 19 482139 1

Printed in China

This book is printed on paper from certified and well-managed sources

ACKNOWLEDGEMENTS

Daisy Robin and Mouse illustrated by: Michael Emmerson/Advocate

Back cover photograph: Oxford University Press building/David Fisher

Other illustrations by: Maria Bogade pp.8, 13, 18, 23, 28, 38, 43; Marta Costa/
Plum Pudding pp.4, 7, 9, 12, 14, 17, 19, 24, 27, 29, 32, 34, 39, 42, 44, 46, 47, 48,
49, 50, 51, 89, 91; Mark Ruffle pp.6, 11, 16, 21, 26, 31, 41, Units 1–8 pop-outs

*The Publishers would also like to thank the following for their kind permission to
reproduce photographs and other copyright material:* Alamy Images: pp.6 (The Chair
and the Pipe by Vincent Van Gogh), 16 (train/Matthew Clarke), Unit 1 popout
(The Chair and the Pipe by Vincent Van Gogh); Corbis: pp.6 The Parisian
Novels (The Yellow Books) by Vincent Van Gogh © Corbis, Unit 1 popout
Van Gogh's Bedroom at Arles by Vincent Van Gogh © Christie's Images, 6 and 7
The Parisian Novels (The Yellow Books) by Vincent Van Gogh © Corbis, Unit 1 popout
Images, Van Gogh's Bedroom at Arles by Vincent Van Gogh © Christie's
pp.11 (snowy hands/Geri Lavrov/Photographer's Choice, eating strawberry/
Alain Caste/StockFood Creative); Getty:
Creative), 16 (taxi/Dave King/Dorling Kindersley); Oxford University Press:
pp.11 (child smelling flower, child looking at ladybird, child listening to
piano), 33 (plane, boat, bus, car), 24 (wellington boots, hat, sweatshirt, gloves),
36 (eggs, honey, milk and cheese, cows, hens, bees)

**The publishers advise that project work involving cutting and
sticking should be carried out under the supervision of an adult.**

Hello!

Robin's new words

Let's count ...

1   2   3   4   5   6   7   8   9   10

- Who can you see? Point and say.
- Join the dots and say the numbers.
- Where's Mouse? Find and colour.

Numbers 1–10 song

1, 2, 3, 4, 5,
Come on, count,
Count with me.
6, 7, 8, 9, 10,
Come on, count,
Count with me.

1, 2, 3, 4, 5,
Come on, count,
Count with me.
6, 7, 8, 9, 10,
Come on, count,
Count with me.

Come on, count,
Count with me.

- Sing the Numbers 1–10 song.

Hello!

Daisy's new words

What colour is it?

purple   green   yellow   red   pink   brown   black   grey   orange   blue

- Point to and say the colours and the numbers.
- Look and colour by numbers.
- What's the weather like? Point and say.

Colours song

Red, red, red, red and yellow,
Green, green, green, green and blue,
Pink, pink, pink, pink and orange,
Grey, grey, grey, grey and brown.

Point to something black,
Point to something white,
Point to something purple!

Point to something black,
Point to something white,
Point to something purple!

- Sing the Colours song.

Hello!

Daisy and Robin's words

apples   flowers   pears   birds

- What can you see? Point and say.
- Count and write the numbers.
- What's the weather like? Point and say.

Weather song

Sunny, sunny, sunny,
Windy, windy, windy,
Rainy, rainy, rainy,
Cloudy, cloudy, cloudy.

Look outside,
What's the weather like?

Today it's (windy),
Today it's (windy),
Today it's (windy).

- Sing the Weather song.

Unit 1 I want to be a teacher

Robin's new words

pencil   book   rubber   scissors   glue   crayons

- Look and stick the classroom stickers.
- Draw and colour your teacher.

Classroom song

Tune: Girls and boys come out to play

This is my teacher,
Listen and look!
This is my pencil,
This is my book.

This is my rubber,
My scissors and glue.
These are my crayons,
Green, red and blue.

(Repeat song)

- Sing the Classroom song.

4

   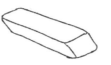

Unit 1

Story

One rainy day, Robin and Daisy are playing with the dressing up box.
'I want to be a **teacher**,' says Robin.
'I want to be a **teacher**, too,' says Daisy.
Robin puts on his teacher costume.
Daisy puts on her teacher costume.
And off they go …

Robin and Daisy are in a school. They can see lots of pupils: Robot, Doll, Superhero, Monster, Monkey and Elephant.
But they can't see a **teacher**.
'Hello,' says Robin. 'Where's your teacher?'
'We haven't got a teacher,' say the pupils.

Robin has an idea.
'Have you got a **pencil** and a **rubber**?' asks Robin.
'I've got a pencil,' says Robot.
'I've got a rubber,' says Doll.
'We've all got a pencil and a rubber, but we haven't got a teacher,' say the pupils.

'Have you got a **crayon** and a **book**?' asks Robin.
'I've got a crayon,' says Superhero.
'I've got a book,' says Monster.
'We've all got a crayon and a book, but we haven't got a teacher,' say the pupils.

'Have you got **scissors** and **glue**?' asks Robin.
'I've got scissors,' says Monkey.
'I've got glue,' says Elephant.
'We've all got scissors and glue, but we haven't got a teacher,' say the pupils.

'I can be your teacher!' says Robin. 'Let's play a game.'
He covers up the **pencil**, **rubber**, **crayon**, **book**, **scissors** and **glue**.

Look at the tray!
'What's missing?' asks Robin.
'The **pencil**,' says Robot.
'The **crayon**,' says Superhero.
'The **glue**,' says Monkey.
'Well done!' says Daisy.

Now it's time to say Goodbye.
'Let's sing the Goodbye song,' says Robin.
So, Robot, Doll, Superhero, Monster, Monkey and Elephant all sing the Goodbye song.
'**Goodbye**,' say Robin and Daisy.
'**Goodbye**, Teacher,' say the pupils.

- Point to and say the classroom items.

- Remember and draw the classroom items in the picture.

- Where's Mouse? Find and point.

5

Picture smart

bed	table	picture	chair

- Look and ✔ or ✘.
- Draw a picture of your bed.

Pictures song

You can draw a picture
Of anything you see.
Look at these pictures,
1, 2, 3!

A bed and a table,
Five pictures, two chairs.
Lots of books
And a chair.

(Repeat song)

- Sing the Pictures song.

Unit 1

Portfolio

Show what you can do

- Point and say.
- Draw yourself.
- Colour the classroom items to match your own.
- Show your teacher.

Notes

Unit

At nursery school

Shall we ...?

pick up the pencils   clean the board   collect the books

- Let's tidy up! Look and circle the helpful actions.
- Point to and say the helpful actions.

Tidy up song 2
Tune: Camptown races

Pick up the pencils   *Tidy up today,*   *Collect the books*   *Tidy up today,*
And clean the board,   *Tidy up today,*   *And clean the board,*   *Tidy up today,*
Tidy, Tidy!   *Pick up the pencils*   *Tidy, Tidy!*   *Collect the books*
Pick up the pencils   *And clean the board,*   *Collect the books*   *And clean the board,*
And clean the board,   *Tidy up today!*   *And clean the board,*   *Tidy up today!*
Tidy up today!   *Tidy up today!*

- Sing the Tidy up song 2.

Unit 2 I want to be a dancer

Daisy's new words

arms   head   body   legs   feet   hands

- Look and stick the body stickers.
- Listen to the parts of the body. Look and say the colours.
- Circle the girls in red and the boys in blue.

Body song
Tune: American marching cadence

Wave your arms, copy me,
Wave your arms, copy me,
Nod your head, 1 2 3!
Nod your head, 1 2 3!

Turn your body round and round,
Turn your body round and round,
Move your legs up and down!
Move your legs up and down!

Stamp your feet and shout for fun,
Stamp your feet and shout for fun,
Clap your hands, everyone!
Clap your hands, everyone!

- Sing the Body song.

Unit 2

Story

One cloudy day, Daisy and Robin are playing
with the dressing up box.
'I want to be a **dancer**,' says Daisy.
'I want to be a **dancer**, too,' says Robin.
Daisy puts on her dancer costume.
Robin puts on his dancer costume.
And off they go …

Daisy and Robin are in the dance show tonight.
Oh, no! Look at their **feet**!
'Where are my shoes?' asks Daisy.
'I don't know,' says Robin. 'Where are *my* shoes?'

Daisy and Robin see some shoes.
'**Look**! Here are some red shoes,' says Daisy.
'Here are some black shoes,' says Robin.
Daisy and Robin put on the shoes.

The shoes are magic!
'Look at my **feet**,' says Daisy. 'They're dancing.'
'My **legs** are moving,' says Robin.

Daisy and Robin dance and dance.
'Look at my **head**,' says Daisy.
'My **body**'s turning round and round,' says Robin.

Daisy and Robin dance and dance.
'Look at my **arms**,' says Daisy.
'My **hands** are clapping,' says Robin.

It's time for the dance show!
Daisy and Robin dance and dance.
They stamp their **feet**. They move their **legs**.
They move their **heads**. They turn their **bodies** round and round.
They move their **arms**. They clap their **hands**.
They are fantastic and everyone claps.

Daisy and Robin dance and dance, but now it's time
to go home. They take off the magic shoes.
'**Goodbye**, red shoes,' says Daisy.
'**Goodbye**, black shoes,' says Robin.

- Where's Mouse? Find and point.
- Look and ✔ the picture from the story.
- Look and circle 5 more differences in Picture 2.
- Point to and say the differences.

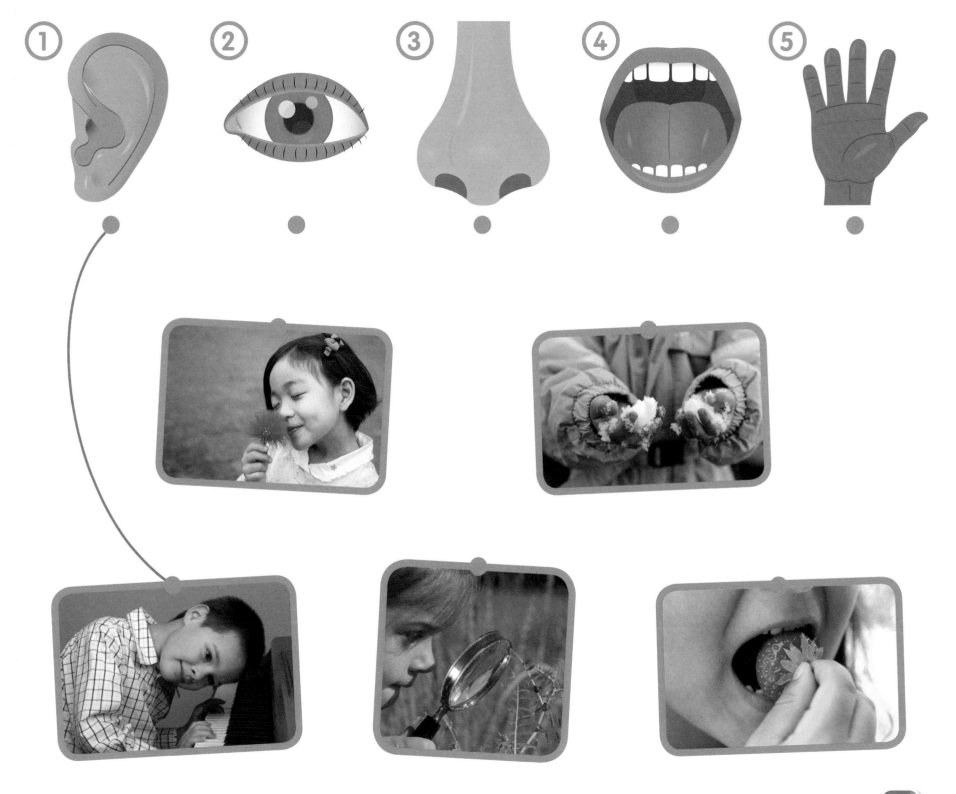

Unit 2

Body smart

| hear | see | smell | taste | touch |

- Point to and say the parts of the body.
- Match the parts of the body to the senses.
- Point to and say the senses.

Five senses song

I've got five senses,
1 2 3 4 5! (Repeat x2)

I can hear with my ears,
I can hear.
I can see with my eyes,
I can see.
I can smell with my nose,
I can smell.

I can taste with my mouth,
I can taste.
I can touch with my hands,
I can touch.

I've got five senses,
1 2 3 4 5! (Repeat x2)

- Sing the Five senses song.

Unit 2

Portfolio

⭐ **Show what you can do**

- Draw yourself dancing.
- Point to and say the parts of the body.
- Point to *touch*. Point to *hear*.
- Show your teacher.

Notes

Unit

At nursery school

Can you ...?

stamp your feet   nod your head   bend your legs

- Point to and say the actions.
- Match the actions and colour the T-shirts.

Dance class song

Can you do the boogie woogie?
Dance, dance, dance!
Can you do the boogie woogie?
Dance, dance, dance!

Stamp, stamp, stamp your feet,
Do the boogie woogie
And stamp your feet!

Nod, nod, nod your head,
Do the boogie woogie
And nod your head!

Bend, bend, bend your legs,
Do the boogie woogie
And bend your legs!

Can you do the boogie woogie?
Dance, dance, dance!
Can you do the boogie woogie?
Dance, dance, dance!

- Sing the Dance class song.

Unit 3 I want to be a pilot

Robin's new words

| bus | taxi | car | plane | train | boat |

- Colour the water blue.
- Look and stick the vehicles stickers.
- Point to and make the noise for each vehicle.

Vehicles song

Tune: When Johnny comes marching home

Brrm! Brrm! Here's a bus,
A taxi and a car.
Brrm! Brrm! Here's a bus,
A taxi and a car.

Zoom! Zoom! Here's a plane,
Chuff! Chuff! Here's a train,
Splash! Splash! Here's a boat
And now we're home again.

(Repeat song)

- Sing the Vehicles song.

Unit 3

Story

One sunny day, Robin and Daisy are playing with the dressing up box.
'I want to be a **pilot**,' says Robin.
'I want to be a **pilot**, too,' says Daisy.
Robin puts on his pilot costume.
Daisy puts on her pilot costume.
And off they go …

Robin and Daisy are at a fair. They see a **plane**.
'Look! A plane,' says Robin. 'Let's go!'
They jump into the plane and fly up into the sky.

'Look at the fair!' says Robin. 'Look at the **cars**!'
'And look at the **boats** on the lake!' says Daisy.
But where are the people? The fair is empty.
'Let's tell everyone about the fair,' says Robin.

Robin and Daisy see some people.
'There's a fair near the lake,' calls Robin.
'A fair?' say the people. 'Hurray! Let's go by **train**.'
And off they go.

Robin and Daisy see a teacher and some children.
'There's a fair near the lake,' calls Daisy.
'A fair?' say the teacher and the children.
'Hurray! Let's go by **bus**.'
And off they go.

Robin and Daisy see a family.
'There's a fair near the lake,' calls Robin.
'A fair?' says the family. 'Hurray! Let's go by **taxi**.'
And off they go.

Everyone is at the **fair**.
Robin flies up and down and round and round.
'Welcome to the fair,' calls Robin. 'Have a lovely time!'

Everyone has a lovely time at the fair, but now it's time to go home.
'**Goodbye**,' say Robin and Daisy.
'**Goodbye**,' say the people.
'Thank you for telling us about the fair.'

- Point to and say the vehicles.
- Let's go to the fair! Trace the route by bus, train and taxi.
- Remember and colour the bus, train and taxi.
- Where's Mouse? Find and point.

1

2

3

4

5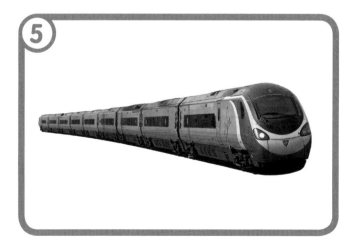

6

Nature smart

air	land	sea

- Point to and say the vehicles.
- Look and circle *air*, *land* or *sea*.

Air, land and sea song
Tune: The Skye boat song

This is a plane, it travels by air,
In the sky it goes.
This is a car, it travels by land,
On the road it goes.

This is a boat, it travels by sea,
Far away from me.
Travelling, travelling far away,
By air and land and sea.

- Sing the Air, land and sea song.

Unit 3

Portfolio

Show what you can do

- Point and say.
- Draw yourself in your favourite vehicle.
- Point to *air*, *land* and *sea*.
- Show your teacher.

Notes

Unit

At nursery school

How do you come to school?

(I come by) car   (I come by) bike   (I) walk

- Look and count how the children come to school. Write the numbers.
- Point and say how you come to school.

Getting to school song
Tune: Michael Finnegan

How do you come to school?
How do you come to school?
How do you come to school
Every day?

I come by car to school,
I come by car to school,
I come by car to school
Every day.

I come by bike to school,
I come by bike to school,
I come by bike to school
Every day.

I walk to school,
I walk to school,
I walk to school
Every day.

How do you come to school?
How do you come to school?
How do you come to school
Every day?

- Sing the Getting to school song.

Unit 4   I want to be a builder

Daisy's new words

| house   roof   floor   window   door   walls |

- Look and stick the house stickers.
- Find and circle the house picture.
- Look and count all the windows and doors you can see.

House song
Tune: Wind the bobbin up

It's a happy house,
It's a happy house,
Clap, clap, clap with Mouse!

It's a happy house,
It's a happy house,
Clap, clap, clap with Mouse!

Point to the roof,
Point to the floor,
Point to the window,
Point to the door,
Point to the walls, 1, 2, 3,
Point to Daisy, Robin and me! (Repeat x2)

- Sing the House song.

Story

One cloudy day, Daisy and Robin are playing with the dressing up box.
'I want to be a **builder**,' says Daisy.
'I want to be a **builder**, too,' says Robin.
Daisy puts on her builder costume.
Robin puts on his builder costume.
And off they go …

Daisy and Robin are at Elf's **house**.
'Look at all the bricks,' says Daisy.
'What shall we build?'
'I don't know,' says Robin. 'Here's Elf. Hello, Elf!'
'Look out!' shouts Daisy.

CRAAAASH!
Oh dear! Now Elf hasn't got a house. She's sad.
'I'm sorry, Elf,' says Robin.
'Don't worry, Elf,' says Daisy. 'We'll build a new house for you.'

Daisy and Robin start to build the new house.
They build four yellow **walls**.
'Look at your new house,' says Daisy.
'It's great,' says Elf, 'but where's the door, and where are the windows? Don't forget the door and the windows!'
'Oops,' say Daisy and Robin.

Daisy and Robin build one red **door** and two white **windows** for the house.
'Look at your new house,' says Daisy.
'It's great,' says Elf, 'but where's the floor? Don't forget the floor!'
'Oops,' say Daisy and Robin.

Daisy and Robin build a brown **floor** for the house.
'Look at your new house,' says Daisy.
'It's great,' says Elf, 'but where's the roof? Don't forget the roof!'
'Oops,' say Daisy and Robin.

Daisy and Robin build a black **roof** for the house.
'Look at your new house now,' says Daisy.
'It's completely finished.'
'Thank you. It's fantastic!' says Elf. 'Come in and have a drink.'

Daisy and Robin have a drink with Elf, but now it's time to go home. They wave goodbye to Elf in her new house with the yellow walls, red door, white windows, brown floor and black roof.
'**Goodbye**,' say Daisy and Robin.
'**Goodbye**,' says Elf.

- Remember and colour the parts of the house from the story.
- Number in order.
- Where's Mouse? Find and point.

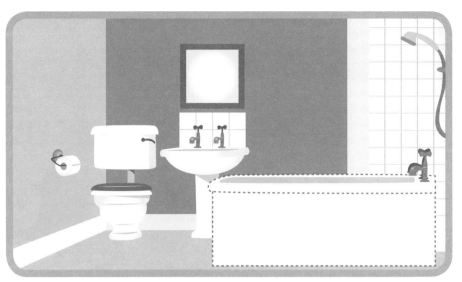

Unit

Self smart

| bathroom | kitchen | living room | bedroom |

- Point to and say the rooms.
- Trace and complete the rooms.
- Match the family to the rooms. Look and colour.

Rooms song

I wash in the bathroom,
The bathroom, the bathroom,
I wash in the bathroom,
Splash, splash, splash!

I eat in the kitchen,
The kitchen, the kitchen,
I eat in the kitchen,
Munch, munch, munch!

I play in the living room,
The living room, the living room,
I play in the living room,
Fun, fun, fun!

I sleep in the bedroom,
The bedroom, the bedroom,
I sleep in the bedroom,
Snore, snore, snore!

- Sing the Rooms song.

Unit 4

Portfolio

Show what you can do

- Draw your house.
- Talk about your house.
- Show your teacher.

Notes

X

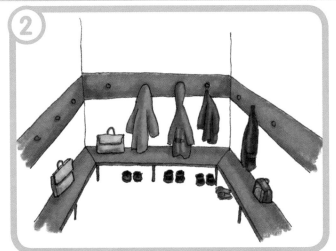

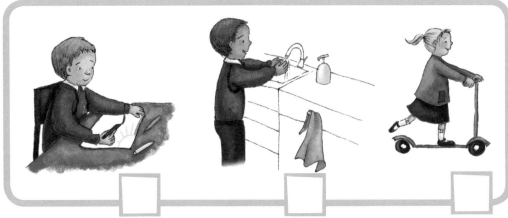

Unit

At nursery school

Where are you?

(In the) playground   (In the) cloakroom   (In the) classroom

- Point to and say the places in school.
- Look and ✔ or ✘.

School places song

Where are you?
Where are you?
In the playground,
In my school.

Where are you?
Where are you?
In the cloakroom,
In my school.

Where are you?
Where are you?
In the classroom,
In my school.

- Sing the School places song.

Unit 5 I want to be a farmer

Robin's new words

| jumper | trousers | hat | boots | socks | gloves |

- Look and stick the clothes stickers.
- Draw the eyes, nose and mouth on the girl and the boy.

Clothes song
Tune: Heads, shoulders, knees and toes

My jumper, my trousers and my hat,
My hat.
My jumper, my trousers and my hat,
My hat.
My boots, my socks and my gloves.
My jumper, my trousers and my hat,
My hat.

(Repeat song)

- Sing the Clothes song.

Unit 5

Story

One sunny day, Robin and Daisy are playing with the dressing up box.
'I want to be a **farmer**,' says Robin.
'I want to be a **farmer**, too,' says Daisy.
Robin puts on his farmer costume.
Daisy puts on her farmer costume.
And off they go …

Robin and Daisy are at a farm.
'Wow! Look at the **strawberries**,' says Robin.
'They're very big.'
But, oh dear! The birds are eating the strawberries.

Robin and Daisy see a scarecrow. He's **sad**.
'What's the matter?' asks Robin.
'I'm not a good scarecrow,' says the scarecrow.
'My clothes are too old. Look, the birds are eating the strawberries.'

'We've got lots of clothes,' says Robin.
'I know!' says Daisy. 'Let's give them to the scarecrow.'
So, Robin takes off his **trousers** and Daisy takes off her **hat**.
'Put on these trousers,' says Robin.
'Put on this hat,' says Daisy.

Daisy takes off her **jumper** and her **gloves**.
'Put on this jumper and these gloves,' says Daisy.
The scarecrow puts on the jumper and the gloves, and some birds fly away.
'That's better,' says Robin.

Robin takes off his **boots** and his **socks**.
'Put on these socks and these boots,' says Robin.
The scarecrow puts on the socks and the boots, and some more birds fly away.
'That's better,' says Robin.

The scarecrow has lots of new clothes.
'Look at my **trousers**, my **hat**, my **jumper**, my **gloves**, my **socks** and my **boots**,' says the scarecrow.
All the birds fly away.
'Hurray!' say Robin and Daisy.

The birds aren't eating the strawberries now!
The scarecrow is a good scarecrow.
He's happy.
'**Goodbye**,' say Robin and Daisy.
'**Goodbye**,' says the scarecrow.
'And thank you!'

- Point and say *happy* or *sad*.

- Remember and draw the birds in the right picture.

- Remember and colour the scarecrow's new clothes.

- Where's Mouse? Find and point.

 4

Nature smart

| winter | spring | summer | autumn |

- Point to and say the clothes and the seasons.
- Find and write the number.

Seasons song

Tune: Let everyone clap hands like me

It's winter, it's winter, hurray!
It's winter, it's winter, hurray!
Put on your gloves
And come out to play,
It's winter, it's winter, hurray!

It's spring, it's spring, hurray!
It's spring, it's spring, hurray!
Put on your boots
And come out to play,
It's spring, it's spring, hurray!

It's summer, it's summer, hurray!
It's summer, it's summer, hurray!
Put on your hat
And come out to play,
It's summer, it's summer, hurray!

It's autumn, it's autumn, hurray!
It's autumn, it's autumn, hurray!
Put on your jumper
And come out to play,
It's autumn, it's autumn, hurray!

- Sing the Seasons song.

Unit 5

Portfolio

Show what you can do

- Circle your favourite season.
- Draw yourself and your clothes for your favourite season.
- Show your teacher.

Notes

Unit

At nursery school

What are these?

carrots   potatoes   tomatoes   beans

- Point to and say the vegetables.

- Look and colour.

- Count the vegetables and write the number.

Vegetables song

Tune: For he's a jolly good fellow

What are these?	*What are these?*	*What are these?*	*What are these?*
Carrots!	*Potatoes!*	*Tomatoes!*	*Beans!*
What are these?	*What are these?*	*What are these?*	*What are these?*
Carrots!	*Potatoes!*	*Tomatoes!*	*Beans!*
What are these?	*What are these?*	*What are these?*	*What are these?*
Carrots	*Potatoes*	*Tomatoes*	*Beans*
For our lunch today!	*For our lunch today!*	*For our lunch today!*	*For our lunch today!*

- Sing the Vegetables song.

Unit 6 I want to be a sailor

Daisy's new words

turtle   fish   seahorse   shark   octopus   crab

- Look and stick the sea stickers.
- Colour 1 pink, 2 green and 3 orange.

Sea song
Tune: Dance to your daddy

I can see a turtle,
I can see a fish,
Splash, splash, splash,
In the sea!

I can see a seahorse,
I can see a shark,
Splash, splash, splash,
In the sea!

I can see an octopus,
I can see a crab,
Splash, splash, splash,
In the sea!

- Sing the Sea song.

Unit 6

Story

One windy day, Daisy and Robin are playing with the dressing up box.
'I want to be a **sailor**,' says Daisy.
'I want to be a **sailor**, too,' says Robin.
Daisy puts on her sailor costume.
Robin puts on his sailor costume.
And off they go …

Daisy and Robin sail out to sea.
'Look! There's a boat race,' says Daisy.
'Hello,' says a **turtle**. 'Would you like to join the race?'
'Yes, please!' say Daisy and Robin.

Daisy, Robin and Turtle line up for the race.
'Ready, steady, GO!' says **Fish**.
The race begins.

'Look! There's a **crab**,' says Robin.
SPLASH!
Oh, no! Crab is out of the race.
'Come with us, Crab,' says Daisy.
Crab climbs into the boat and they sail on.

'Look! There's an **octopus**,' says Robin.
SPLASH!
Oh, no! Octopus is out of the race.
'Come with us, Octopus,' says Daisy.
Octopus climbs into the boat and they sail on.

'Look! There's a **seahorse**,' says Robin.
SPLASH!
Oh, no! Seahorse is out of the race.
'Come with us, Seahorse,' says Daisy.
Seahorse climbs into the boat and they sail on.

Daisy, Robin and their team cross the finish line.
'Congratulations! You're the winners!' says **Shark**.
'Hurray!' say Daisy, Robin, Turtle, Crab, Octopus and Seahorse.

Daisy and Robin watch more races, but now it's time to go home. They wave goodbye to Turtle, Fish, Crab, Octopus, Seahorse and Shark.
'**Goodbye**,' say Daisy and Robin.
'**Goodbye**,' say the sea animals.

- Point to and say the sea animals.
- Remember and match the sea animals to the right picture.
- Where's Mouse? Find and point.

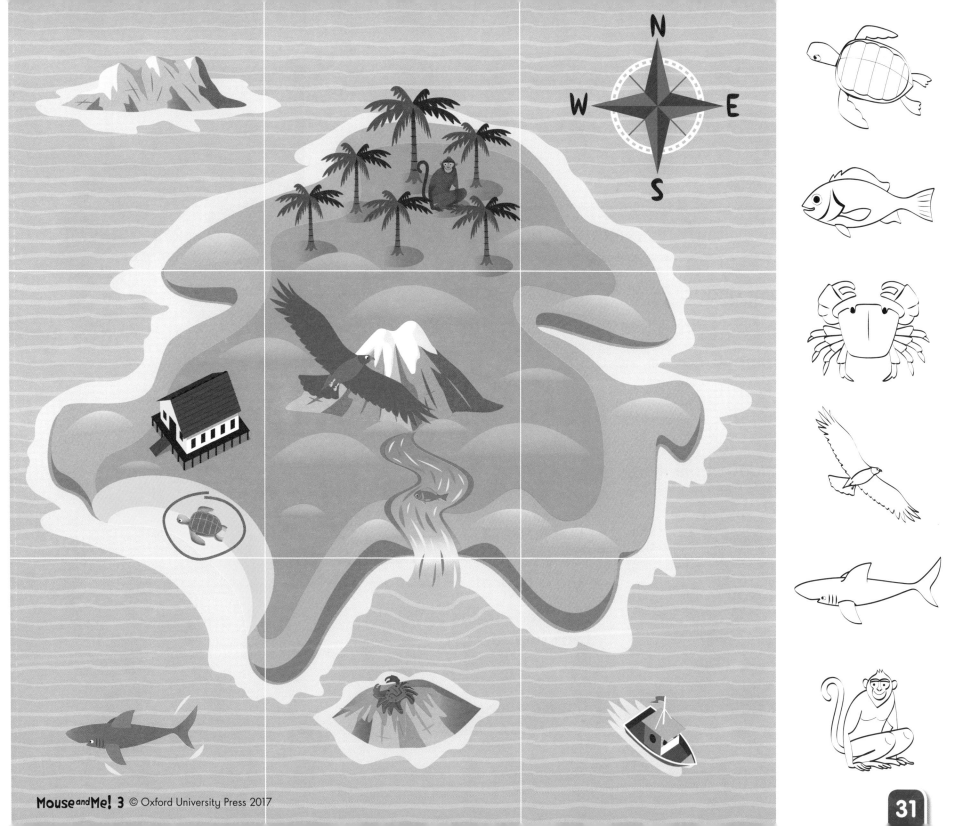

Unit 6

Picture smart

| map island mountain beach |

- Point and say.
- Find and circle the animals on the map.
- Look and colour the animals.

Maps song

Tune: Row, row, row your boat

Look, look at the map,
Look and see!
There's an island
In the sea.
There's an island
In the sea.

Look, look at the map,
Look and see!
There's a river
And a beach.
There's a river
And a beach.

Look, look at the map,
Look and see!
There's a mountain
And some trees.
There's a mountain
And some trees.

Look, look at the map,
Look and see!
There's a house
For you and me!
There's a house
For you and me!

- Sing the Maps song.

Unit 6

Portfolio

Show what you can do

- Draw an island.
- Draw your favourite land animal on the island.
- Draw your favourite sea animal in the sea.
- Talk about your picture. Point and say.
- Show your teacher.

Notes

Unit

At nursery school

What are you making?

A castle   A road   A lake

- Complete the castle.
- Point to the road. Colour the car red.
- Point to the lake. Trace the boat.

Sand play song
Tune: Rig a jig jig

What are you making in the sand,
In the sand, in the sand?
What are you making in the sand?
Dig, dig, dig!

I'm making a castle in the sand,
In the sand, in the sand.
I'm making a castle in the sand,
Dig, dig, dig!

I'm making a road in the sand,
In the sand, in the sand.
I'm making a road in the sand,
Dig, dig, dig!

I'm making a lake in the sand,
In the sand, in the sand.
I'm making a lake in the sand,
Dig, dig, dig!

- Sing the Sand play song.

Unit 7 I want to be a chef

Robin's new words

bread   cheese   butter   ham   egg   salad

- Look and stick the food stickers.
- Look and draw a happy face by the food you like.

Food song
Tune: Do you know the muffin man?

*I like bread
And I like cheese.
I like butter,
A sandwich, please!*

*Ham and egg
And salad, too.
I'm very hungry,
What about you?*

(Repeat song)

- Sing the Food song.

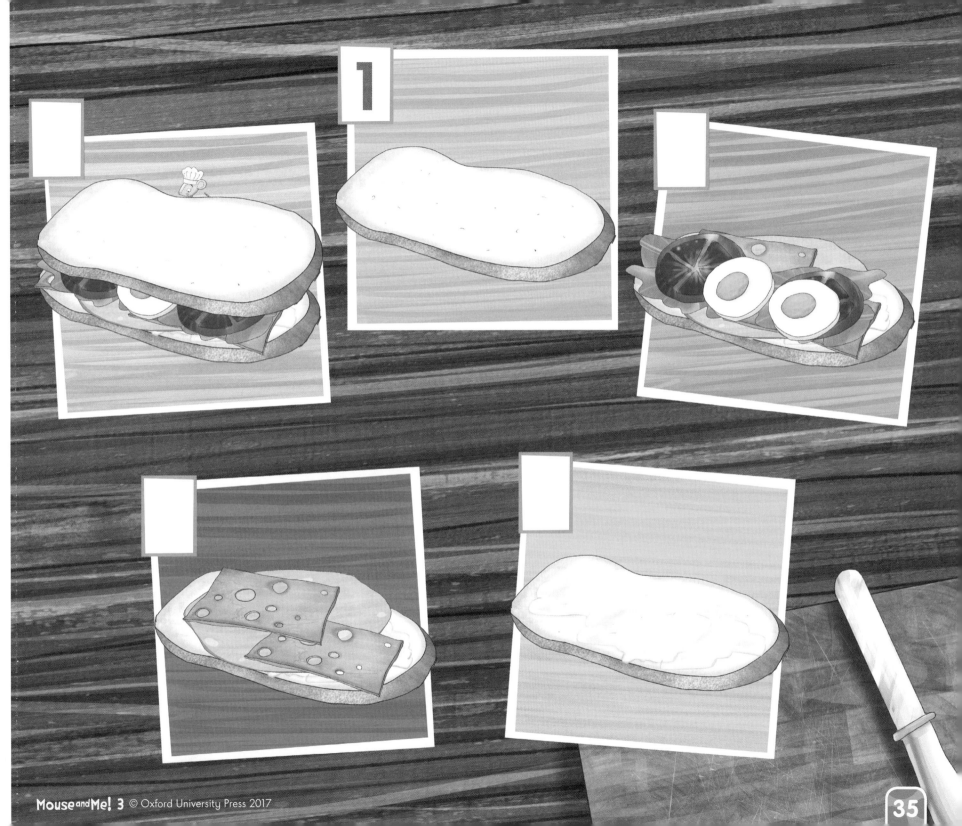

Unit 7

Story

One rainy day, Robin and Daisy are playing with the dressing up box.
'I want to be a **chef**,' says Robin.
'I want to be a **chef**, too,' says Daisy.
Robin puts on his chef costume.
Daisy puts on her chef costume.
And off they go …

Robin and Daisy are in a giant's kitchen.
'I'm hungry,' roars the giant. 'Where's my lunch?'
'Wait, please,' says Robin.
'Give me some **bread**, please, Daisy,' says Robin.
Daisy gives Robin some bread.

'I'm very hungry,' roars the giant. 'Where's my lunch?'
'Wait, please,' says Robin.
'Give me some **butter**, please, Daisy,' says Robin.
Daisy gives Robin some butter.

'I'm very, very hungry,' roars the giant.
'Where's my lunch?'
'Wait, please,' says Robin.
'Give me some **ham** and some **cheese**, please, Daisy,' says Robin.
Daisy gives Robin some ham and some cheese.

'I'm very, very, very hungry,' roars the giant. 'Where's my lunch?'
'Wait, please,' says Robin.
'Give me some **salad** and some **egg**, please, Daisy,' says Robin.
Daisy gives Robin some salad and some egg.

'Where's my lunch?' roars the giant. 'I'm very, very, very, very hungry. WHERE'S MY LUNCH?'
'Here it is,' says Robin. 'A giant sandwich. With **bread**, **butter**, **ham**, **cheese**, **salad** and **egg**.'

The giant opens his **mouth**. He takes a big bite.
'Mmmm!' says the giant. 'Mmmm! It's very good.'
He takes another bite, and another, and another, until the sandwich is all gone.
'Thank you!' says the giant. 'I'm not hungry any more. But I'm sleepy.'

The giant's sleeping!
'Let's go home,' whispers Robin.
Robin and Daisy tiptoe out of the giant's kitchen.
'**Goodbye**,' whisper Robin and Daisy.

- Remember and number in order.

- Point to and say the food.

- Where's Mouse? Find and point.

Unit

Nature smart

| chickens | bees | cows | honey | milk |

- Match the food to the animals.
- Point and say.

Food from animals song

Tune: Oat and beans and barley grow

Eggs come from chickens,
Honey comes from bees,
Milk comes from cows
And so does cheese!

Lots of food,
Munch, munch, munch!
Food from animals
For our lunch!

(Repeat song)

- Sing the Food from animals song.

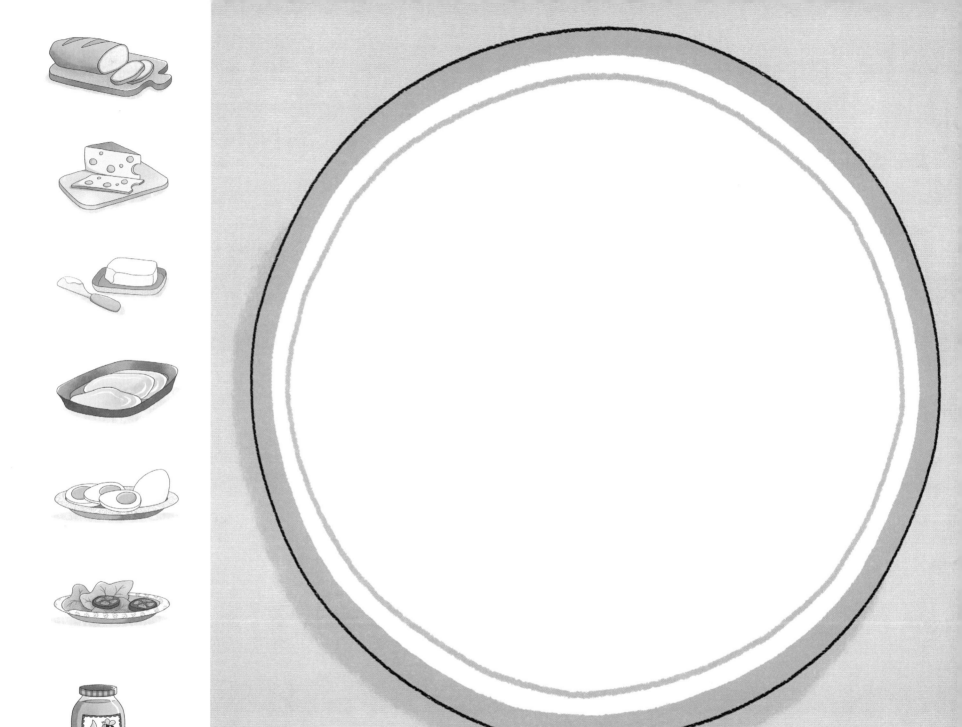

Unit 7

Portfolio

Show what you can do

- Point to and say the food.
- Draw your favourite sandwich. Choose and circle. Then draw.
- Show your teacher.

Notes

Unit

At nursery school

What's for ...?

breakfast   snack   lunch

- Point to and say the meals.
- Look and ✔ the food and drink for each meal.

Meals song
Tune: Waltzing Matilda

What's for breakfast?
What's for breakfast?
What's for breakfast
For us today?
There's bread and milk
And juice and honey,
All for breakfast
For us today!

What's for snack?
What's for snack?
What's for snack
For us today?
There are oranges and pears
And bananas and apples,
All for snack
For us today!

What's for lunch?
What's for lunch?
What's for lunch
For us today?
There's ham and cheese
And egg and salad,
All for lunch
For us today!

- Sing the Meals song.

Unit **8** I want to be a gardener

Daisy's new words

pond	grass	path	leaves	flowers	bench

- Look and stick the garden stickers.
- Count the flowers and write the number.
- Point to and say the animals.

Garden song

Tune: When the saints go marching in

There's a pond,
There's some grass,
There's a path
Where you can walk.
There are some leaves
And some flowers,
There's a bench
Where you can sit!

(Repeat song)

- Sing the Garden song.

Unit 8

Story

One sunny day, Daisy and Robin are playing with the dressing up box.
'I want to be a **gardener**,' says Daisy.
'I want to be a **gardener**, too,' says Robin.
Daisy puts on her gardener costume.
Robin puts on his gardener costume.
And off they go …

Daisy and Robin are in a park.
They can see a snake in the grass, a bird on the bench, and a rabbit on the path.
But the park is a **mess**.

'Let's tidy up the park!' says Daisy.
So, Daisy cuts the **grass** and Robin tidies up the **leaves**.
'Where's the snake?' asks Daisy. 'It isn't in the grass.'
'I don't know,' says Robin.

Next, Daisy paints the **bench** and Robin waters the **flowers**.
'Where's the bird?' asks Daisy. 'It isn't on the bench.'
'I don't know,' says Robin.

Finally, Daisy cleans the **path** and Robin cleans the **pond**.
'Where's the rabbit?' asks Daisy. 'It isn't on the path.'
'I don't know,' says Robin.

The park is tidy now.
'**Hurray**, we've finished!' says Robin.
'Yes, but where are the animals?' says Daisy.

Suddenly, Daisy and Robin hear some music.
'**SURPRISE!**' say the animals.
'Wow! Look!' says Robin.
'Thank you, Daisy; thank you, Robin, for tidying up the park,' says the rabbit. 'It's beautiful.'

Daisy and Robin have a party with the animals, but now it's time to go home. They wave goodbye to the snake, the bird and the rabbit in the beautiful, tidy park.
'**Goodbye**,' say Daisy and Robin.
'**Goodbye**,' say the animals.

- Remember and circle Daisy or Robin for each picture.
- Where's Mouse? Find and point.

40

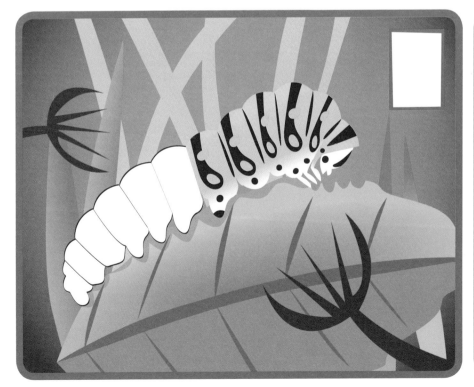

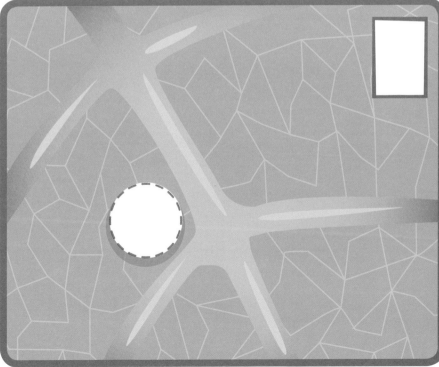

Unit

Nature smart

butterfly	caterpillar	cocoon

- Colour the cocoon.
- Complete the butterfly and the caterpillar.
- Trace the egg.
- Number in order.
- Point and say.

Butterfly life cycle song

Tune: Tommy Thumb

*Butterfly, butterfly
On the leaf,
Butterfly, butterfly
Lays an egg.*

*Caterpillar, caterpillar
Comes out of the egg,
Caterpillar, caterpillar
Eats and eats.*

*Caterpillar, caterpillar
Makes a cocoon,
Butterfly, butterfly
Comes out soon.*

- Sing the Butterfly life cycle song.

Unit 8

Portfolio

Show what you can do

- Draw a garden.
- Point and say.
- Show your teacher.

Notes

Unit

At nursery school

What have you found?

(A) ladybird   (An) ant   (A) spider

- Find and circle the mini beasts in the garden.
- Point to and say the mini beasts.

Mini beasts song

Fly like a ladybird,
Whizz, whizz, whizz!
Walk like an ant,
Pitter patter, pitter patter!
Crawl like a caterpillar,
Crawl, crawl, crawl!
Swing like a spider,
Wheeeeeeee!
And buzz, buzz, buzz,
Buzz like a bee!

(Repeat song)

- Sing the Mini beasts song.

Carnival

Mouse and Me! 3 © Oxford University Press 2017

Carnival

Happy Carnival!

sing　　dance　　mask　　costume

- Point and say.
- Look and circle 6 differences in Picture 2.
- Say *Happy Carnival!*

Carnival song

Five, four, three, two, one!
Happy carnival to everyone!
Put on your costume,
Put on your mask, too.
Happy, happy Carnival to you!
Dance, dance, dance!
Sing, sing, sing!
Dance, dance, dance!
Sing, sing, sing!
Five, four, three, two, one!
Happy Carnival to everyone!

- Sing the Carnival song.

Happy Carnival!

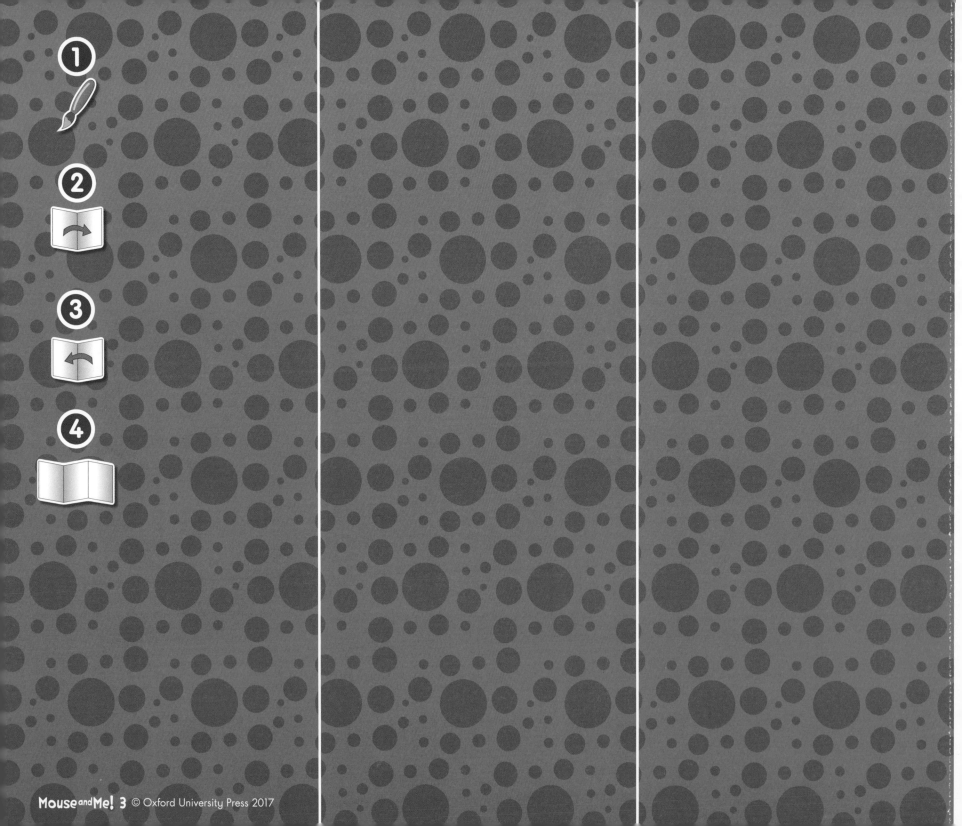

Christmas

46

Christmas

Happy Christmas!

> star   Father Christmas   bell   reindeer

- Point and say.
- Count and write the numbers.

Christmas song

Stars are shining in the sky,
Father Christmas is coming!
Bells are ringing in the night,
The reindeer are flying high.

Put the star on the Christmas tree,
Put the stocking on the fireplace.
Hurry, hurry, say goodnight,
Come on, it's time for bed!

Father Christmas, oh Father Christmas,
Father Christmas is coming soon.
Father Christmas, oh Father Christmas!
It's Christmas for me and you.

Stars are shining in the sky,
Father Christmas is coming!
Bells are ringing in the night,
The reindeer are flying high.

Father Christmas, oh Father Christmas,
Father Christmas is coming soon.
Father Christmas, oh Father Christmas!
It's Christmas for me and you.

- Sing the Christmas song.

46

Happy Christmas!

Easter

Mouse and Me! 3 © Oxford University Press 2017

Easter

Happy Easter!

Easter egg hunt chocolate sweet basket

- Look and complete the Easter pictures.
- Point and say.

Easter song

Easter egg hunt, here's a purple one!
Easter egg hunt, here's a yellow one!
Easter egg hunt, pink and blue,
Chocolate and sweets in my basket now.

Easter egg hunt, here's a purple one!
Easter egg hunt, here's a yellow one!
Easter egg hunt, red and green,
Chocolate and sweets in my basket, see!

Come on let's play together,
Together will be better,
Happy Easter time!

Come on let's play together,
Together will be better,
Happy Easter time!

Happy Easter time!

- Sing the Easter song.

48

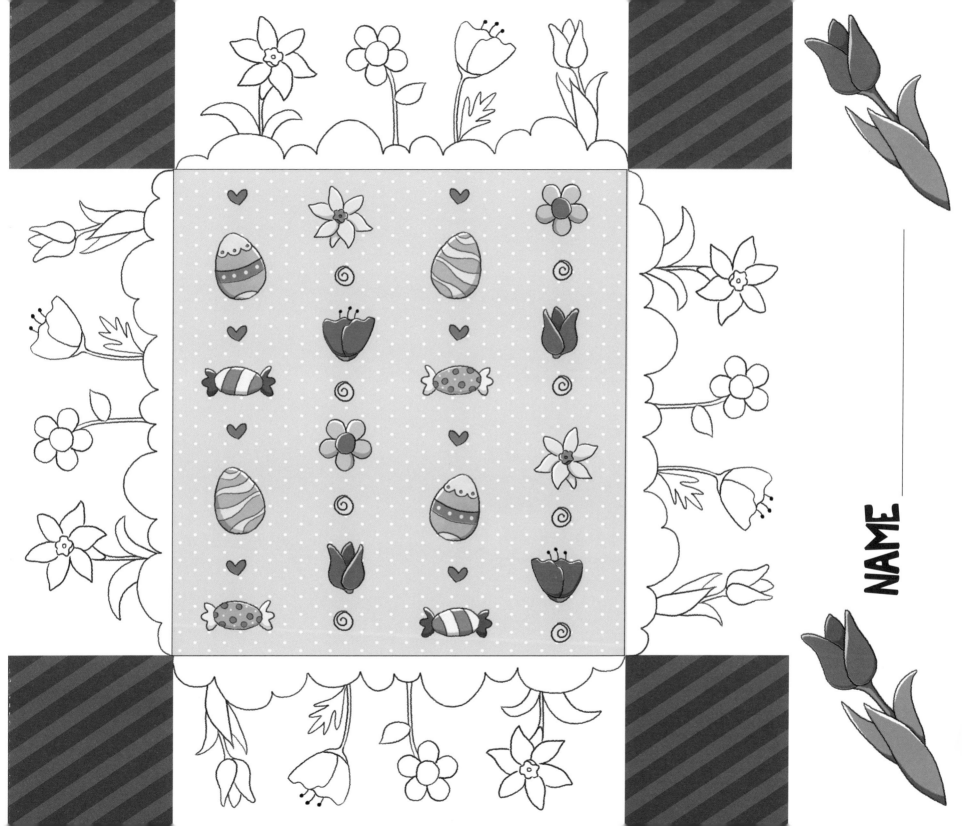

NAME

① ✂

② 📖 ——

③ 🖊

Summer

50

Summer

Summer fair

cakes   flags   parade   queen

- Point to and say the costumes in the parade.
- Find and write the number.

Summer song

Summer fair, summer fair,
Cakes and flags everywhere,
Summer fair, summer fair,
Come and join our fun parade!

Let's say hello
To the queen of the fair,
To the farmer, the sailor,
The pilot.

Summer fair, summer fair,
Cakes and flags everywhere,
Summer fair, summer fair,
Come and join our fun parade!

Let's say hello
To the queen of the fair,
To the dancer, the chef
And the builder.

Summer fair, summer fair,
Cakes and flags everywhere,
Summer fair, summer fair,
Come and join our fun parade!

- Sing the Summer song.

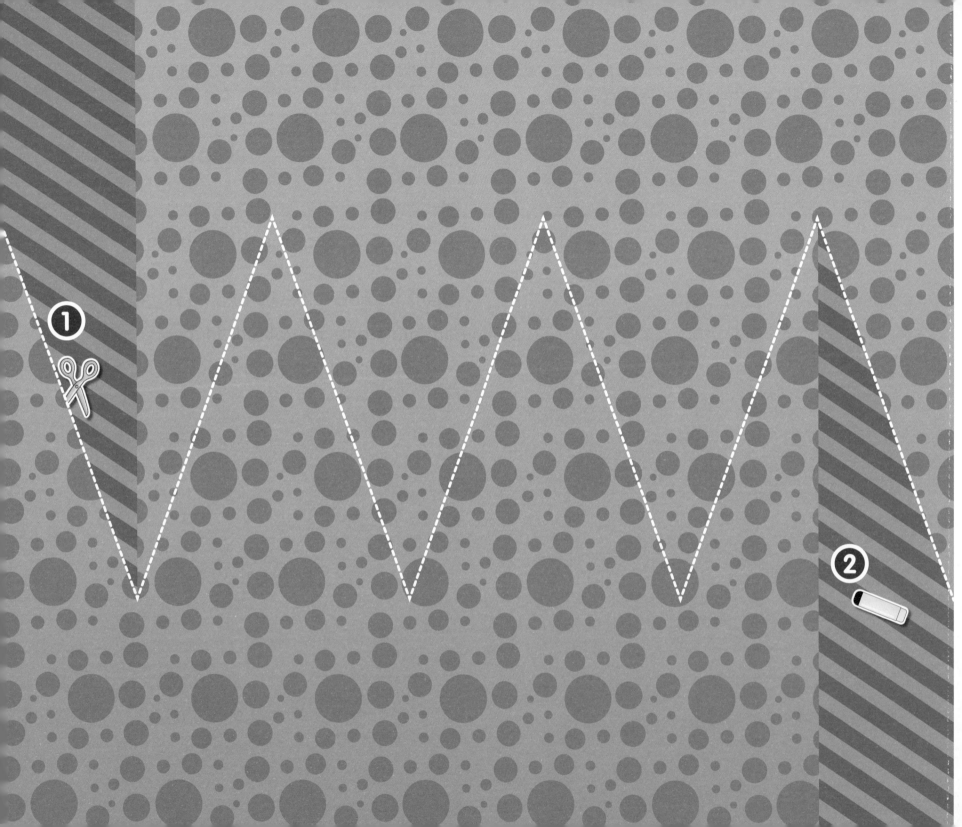

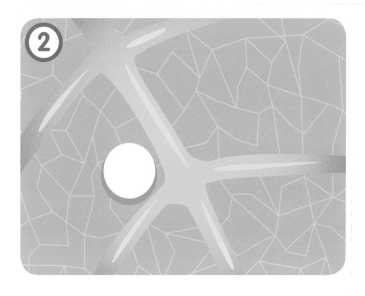

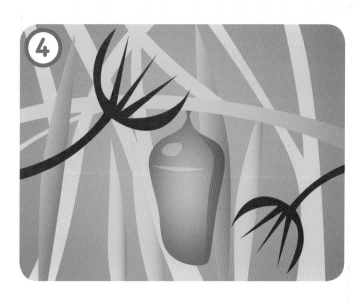

Unit 7 Nature smart Food from animals

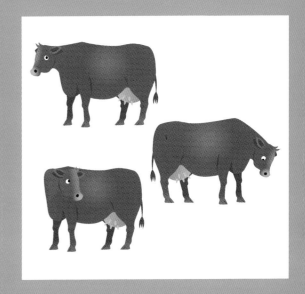

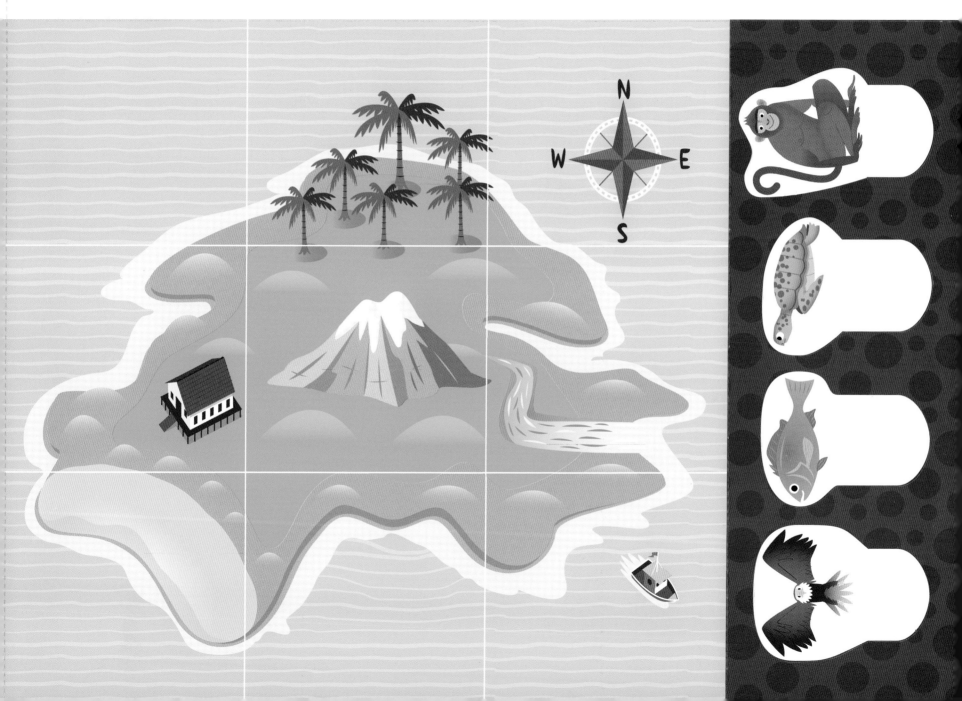

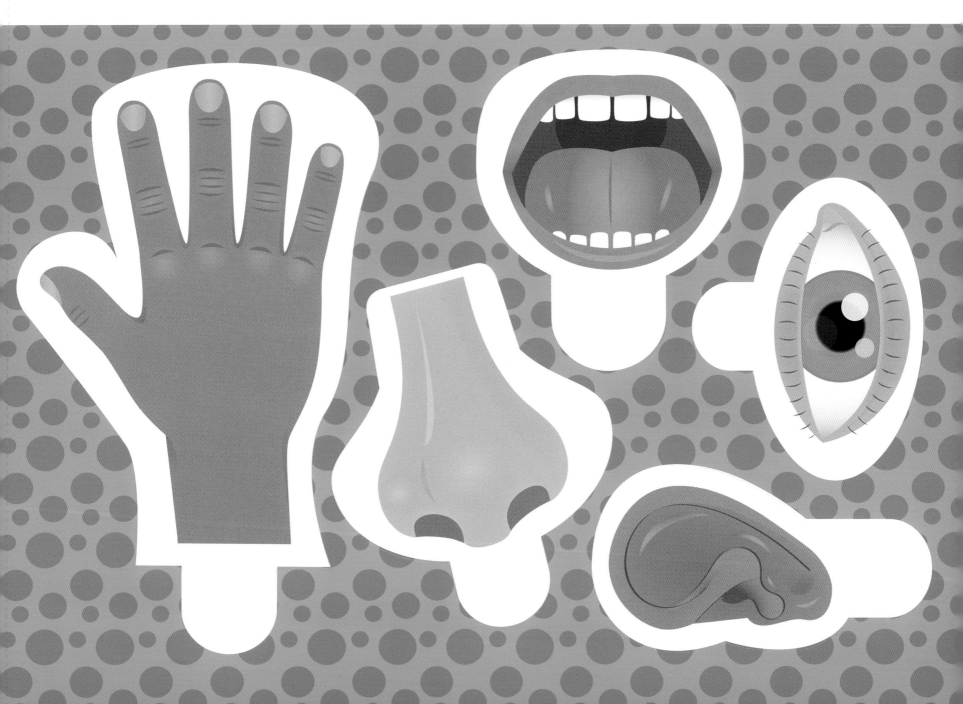

Unit 1

Unit 2

Unit 2

Unit 2

Unit 1

Unit 1

Unit 2

Unit 2

Unit 2

Unit 2

Unit 3

Unit 3

Unit 1

Unit 3

Unit 1

Unit 1

Unit 3

Unit 3

Unit 3

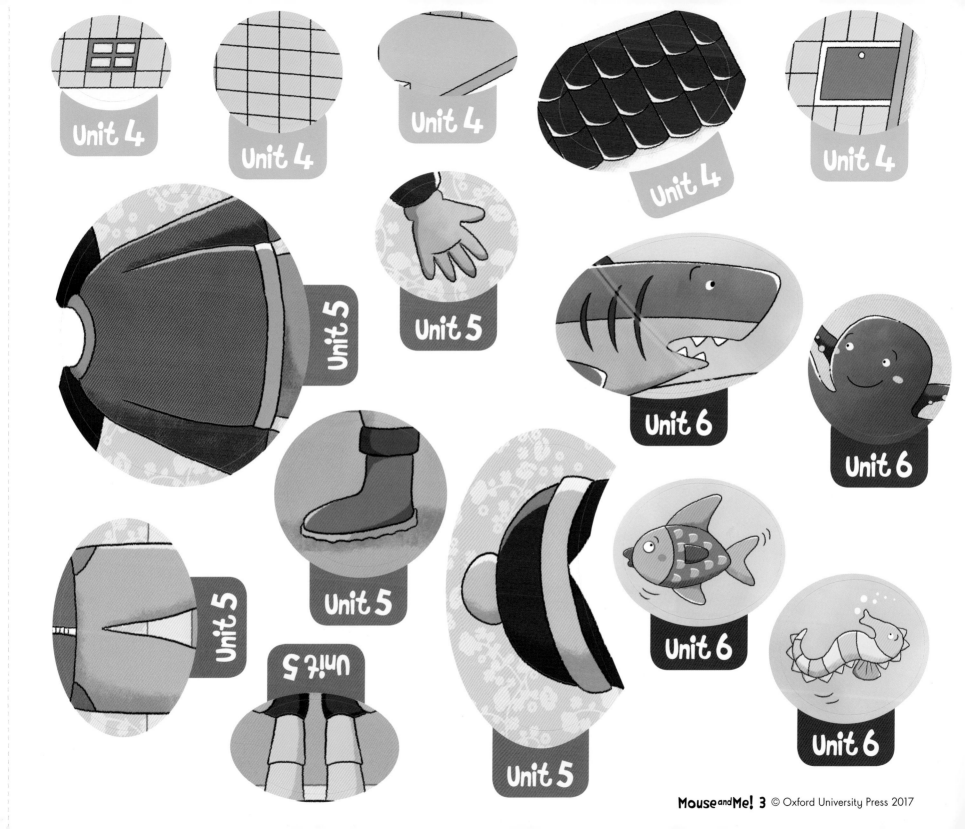

Unit 4

Unit 4

Unit 4

Unit 4

Unit 4

Unit 5

Unit 5

Unit 5

Unit 5

Unit 5

Unit 5

Unit 6

Unit 6

Unit 6

Unit 6

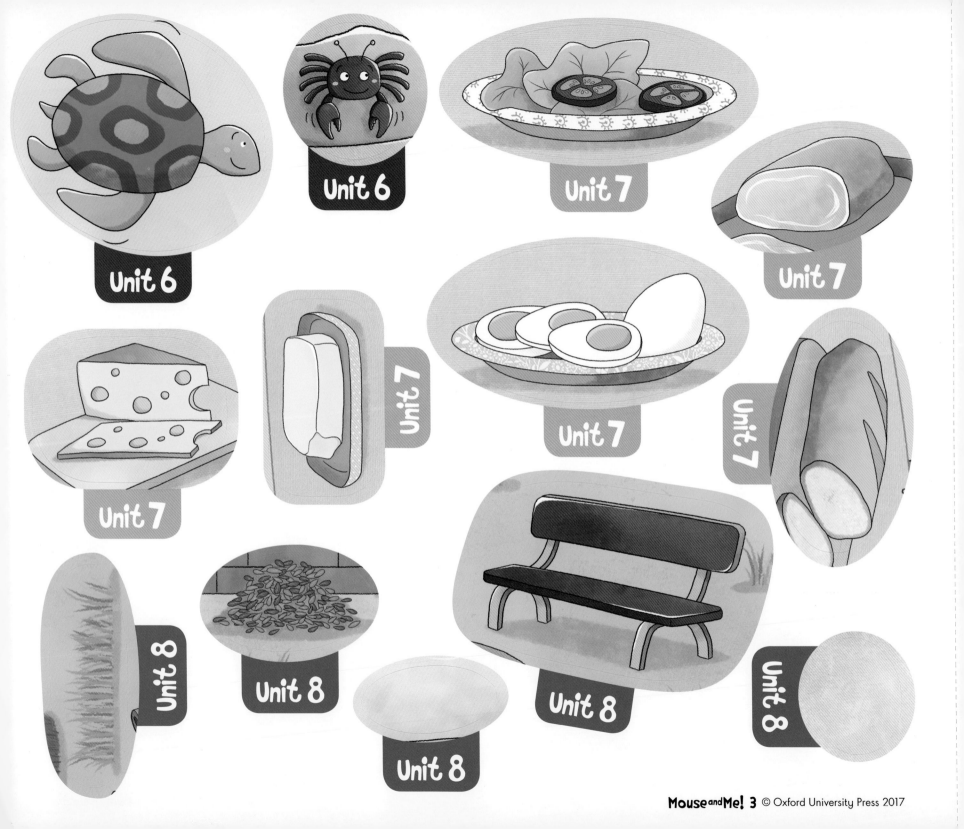

Unit 6

Unit 6

Unit 7

Unit 7

Unit 7

Unit 7

Unit 7

Unit 7

Unit 8

Unit 8

Unit 8

Unit 8

Unit 8

Costume stickers